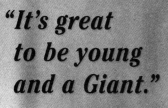

"It's great to be young and a Giant."

—Larry Doyle

David Green

101 Reasons to Love™ the

GIANTS

FOLLOW THE **OAKS**
IN THE **TRIBUNE**

Stewart, Tabori & Chang
New York

Introduction

Thump-smack! Thump-smack! Thump-smack! That was the sound my mother heard day after day back in the mid-1960s, as I honed my fielding skills by bouncing a rubber ball off the wall of our modest little house in the sleepy Southern town of Charlotte, North Carolina. I spent countless hours in that side yard, often playing full nine-inning games by tossing line drives and ground balls off the brick and pop flies off the roof. I would field the grounders and fire them back against the wall, snagging the ball to get the out at first. I'd park myself under the more routine pop flies off the roof and make the catch. Sometimes, if a ball landed just right, it would sail over the chain-link fence that bordered our neighbor's yard for a home run. But every once in a while, I could chase those deep flies down, making a spectacular catch at the fence, to save the day—just like Willie Mays.

I had other favorites, like the Orioles' Brooks Robinson, and the Red Sox' Carl Yastrzemski, but there was no one like the "Say Hey Kid." To me, no one has ever played the game better than Willie Mays.

With my love for baseball came a passion for collecting baseball cards. I would squirrel away every precious coin I found or was given, saving them for that glorious trip to King's Drugs where I would buy as many packs of cards as my savings would allow, hoping beyond hope to find one of baseball's superstars in a pack.

I eventually got them all—except for the one I wanted more than anything in the world, Willie Mays. I'm not talking one season here. I collected cards for years, and I never seemed to come up with a single Mays.

Then, one night, I was at the ballpark with my dad and brother, watching the local minor-league team play, when another kid came by with his stack of cards. He must've had 50 or so with him and many more at home. He let me leaf through them. I was amazed and vividly green with envy to see he had not one but two Willie Mays cards. I couldn't believe it!

I asked him how he had managed to get two, and he said he actually had three. There was another one at home. Three! Are you kidding me? Still, I was 110 percent sure he would never part with one. How could you ever give up a Willie Mays card, no matter how many you had? Nevertheless, I asked him if he would consider trading one. He had three, after all. Even if he traded one, he'd still have two. That was my sales pitch, even though I didn't buy it myself.

Surprisingly, he said sure, if I had the right guy—who could I offer? I threw out some names, knowing none of them were the equal of Mays. Hank Aaron? Got him. Frank Robinson? Got him. Yastrzemski? Got him. Roberto Clemente? Got him.

I was running out of names. My mind kept offering up those four Vic Roznovskys I had sitting at home. Desperate for anyone that might keep the transaction alive, I threw out Tony Oliva. "Tony Oliva?" he said. "You have Tony Oliva?"

"Yeah, I have two of 'em," I answered, not sure if he was interested or incredulous. I mean, Tony Oliva was great and all, but he was no Willie Mays.

"Sure, I'll trade you a Mays for Oliva," he responded excitedly. "I love Oliva."

I was floored. I couldn't believe it. Head-over-heels ecstatic. Overcome with joy.

I got Willie Mays, the greatest player ever to play the game, for Tony Oliva. Straight up. The greatest trade in baseball-card history.

WILLIE
MAYS

OUTFIELD
GIANTS

1 In the Beginning

The long and rich history of the New York Giants began way back in December of 1882. John B. Day, a wealthy tobacco merchant, and his partner, Jim Mutrie, owners of the Metropolitan Exhibition Company, turned down the National League's request to add their New York Metropolitans franchise to the league. Instead, Day and Mutrie agreed to join the American Association, placing the Mets there, and then requested permission to form a new franchise that would play in the National League. The league agreed, and Day and Mutrie founded the New York Gothams. Managed by John Clapp, the Gothams played their first official game on May 1, 1883. To the delight of some 15,000 spectators, including former president Ulysses S. Grant, New York bested the Boston Red Stockings, 7–5, at the original Polo Grounds. The team went on to finish its inaugural season in sixth place with a record of 46–50.

1883 team photo; John B. Day, inset

2 My Giants

Jim Mutrie was running the New York Metropolitans of the American Association when John B. Day asked him to manage the Gothams in 1885. Mutrie brought several of the Mets' best players with him, and the team went on to post a remarkable 85–27 record in just its third season. Even more remarkable, it finished second, two games behind the Chicago White Stockings.

After a dramatic 11th-inning win over Philadelphia, the delighted Mutrie exclaimed, "My big fellows! My giants!" The name caught on, and the team has been known as the Giants ever since.

John McGraw, left,
and Jim Mutrie

3 The Polo Grounds, Part 1

New York played its first game ever, in 1883, on a field that had previously been used as a polo grounds by Manhattan society types. Located at 110th Street and Sixth Avenue in upper Manhattan, the team played here through the 1888 season, when the Giants won their first world championship.

Before the start of the 1889 season, owner John B. Day moved the team uptown, to 155th Street and Eighth Avenue in Harlem, below the cliffs known as Coogan's Bluff. The new grandstand was still under construction when the season started, so the team played its first 25 "home" games in New Jersey and then Staten Island, before moving into the second Polo Grounds. Despite the delay, the Giants won their second consecutive National League pennant that year.

Ed Crane pitched the first no-hitter in Giants history on September 28, a 3–0 victory over the Washington Senators. Crane went on to win four games in the World Series, as the Giants defeated their crosstown rivals, the American Association's Brooklyn Bridegrooms, 6 games to 3.

KEEFE, (P. NEW YORK)

JUDGE & GYPSY QUEEN CIGARETTES

4 A Hall of a Team

The 1885 Giants roster featured six future Hall of Famers: Roger Connor, Buck Ewing, Tim Keefe, Jim O'Rourke, John Montgomery Ward, and Mickey Welch.

Connor held the major-league career home-run record with 138 until it was broken by Babe Ruth in 1921. He was also New York's first batting champ, leading the league with a career-high .371 average.

Many regarded Ewing as the best player of the 19th century. An original member of the Gothams, Ewing batted .306 in 1888, leading New York to its first championship. He followed that by hitting .327 in 1889, as the Giants repeated as World Champions. Ewing was the first catcher to be inducted into the Hall of Fame, in 1939.

"Sir Timothy" Keefe set a major-league record in 1888 by winning 19 consecutive games. He also led the league in wins (35), ERA (1.74), shutouts (8), and strikeouts (335). Keefe pitched four complete-game victories in the World Series, with an ERA of 0.51.

O'Rourke batted over .300 five times in his eight years in New York, including .360 in 1890.

Ward, an accomplished pitcher before joining the Giants, eventually made the switch to short-stop and hit a career-high .338 in 1887 while contributing 111 stolen bases, a franchise record.

"Smiling Mickey" Welch struck out the first nine Cleveland hitters he faced on August 28, 1884, setting a major-league record; the New York Mets' Tom Seaver struck out 10 in a row in 1970.

Welch went on to win 39 games in '84 with 345 strikeouts, while completing 62 of 65 games. He followed that effort by going 44–11 in 1885 with a 1.66 ERA, winning 17 consecutive games in one stretch. Welch won 307 games over the course of his career and was inducted into the Hall of Fame in 1973.

WELCH, P., New Yorks
COPYRIGHT BY GOODWIN & CO., 1888.
OLD JUDGE
CIGARETTE FACTORY.
GOODWIN & CO., New York.

5 Two Titles

It didn't take long for the Giants to establish themselves as one of the premier franchises in baseball. New York won the first of its two consecutive world championships in 1888, behind the pitching of Tim Keefe and the hitting of Roger Connor and Buck Ewing. Keefe won a record 19 starts in a row and 35 overall, while Connor hit 14 home runs and Ewing chipped in with a .306 batting average. The Giants won their first National League pennant by nine games over Chicago, then defeated the St. Louis Browns of the American Association 6 games to 4 in the world championship.

In 1889, the Giants edged the Boston Beaneaters by a single game to earn their second consecutive National League pennant. Tim Keefe and Mickey Welch combined to win 55 games, and Ed Crane threw the franchise's first no-hitter in September. He followed that up by posting a 4–1 record in the World Series, which the Giants won over the Brooklyn Bridegrooms.

6 No Mercy

In June of 1887, the Giants spanked Washington 26–2, and Philadelphia 29–1, in games just four days apart. New York's most lopsided shutout win was a 24–0 pasting of the Buffalo Bisons,   in May 1885.

7 Silent Mike

In his 13-year career with the Giants, soft-spoken Mike Tiernan hit better than .300 seven times, including a career-best .369 in 1896. "Silent Mike" holds the franchise record for triples with 162 and stolen bases with 428. He was the first player in Giants history to hit for the cycle, on August 25, 1888, versus Philadelphia.

8 The Hoosier Thunderbolt

Amos Rusie brought his blazing fastball to the Giants in 1890 at the age of 18. In his rookie season, the "Hoosier Thunderbolt" led the league with a career-high 341 strikeouts. In 1891–94, he topped 30 wins each year, with a career-high 36 in '94. Rusie is third all-time in both complete games (372) and strikeouts (1,835), in only eight seasons with the Giants. In 1891, he became the youngest pitcher to throw a no-hitter, when he blanked the Brooklyn Bridegrooms 6–0 at the age of 20 years, 2 months.

9 The Hitman

Giants fans weren't happy in 1893 when the team traded popular catcher Buck Ewing for young and unproven infielder George Davis. Their dismay quickly turned to delight as Davis fashioned a franchise-record 33-game hitting streak in August and early September of that same year. He hit .355 for the season with a then-franchise-record 27 triples. Davis followed that by hitting .352 in '94. In all, he posted nine consecutive seasons with the Giants in which he hit better than .300.

Amos Rusie

10 The Polo Grounds, Part 2

Giants owner John B. Day moved his team to Brotherhood Park in 1891. When the ballpark burned in 1911, reconstruction began immediately, with additional stands built over several years. The new Polo Grounds was unique among the major-league parks. Its enclosed horseshoe shape created a playing field with very short distances down the lines, but straightaway center field was an almost unreachable 483 feet. The odd dimensions and varying angles made for many exciting and unpredictable moments. From 1911 to 1957, the Giants won 13 pennants and four World Series titles. When the Polo Grounds was demolished in 1964, the demolition crew wore Giants jerseys to commemorate the event.

11 Get 'Em While They're Hot

Legend has it the term "hot dog" originated at the Polo Grounds in the early 1900s. On a chilly April day, concessionaire Harry M. Stevens offered a warm alternative to ice cream by selling sausages on rolls he called "red-hot dachshund sausages." *New York Journal* cartoonist Ted Dorgan depicted the popular culinary delights in a published illustration. Unsure how to spell dachshund, he dubbed the creation "hot dog." The name caught on, and ever since, hot dogs have been a staple at ballparks.

Original artwork by Andy Jurinko

John T. Brush

12 The Worst Owner Ever

Andrew Freedman, known to many as "the worst owner ever," nearly ran the Giants into the ground in his short term as owner. In a mere eight seasons, 1895–1902, Freedman ran through 12 different managers, including Hall of Famer Cap Anson—who left after just 22 games, unable to endure Freedman's rule. But the lowlight of Freedman's reign had to be the hiring of Harvey Watkins, an actor and circus performer with no previous baseball experience. Somehow, the Giants managed to go 18–17 under Watkins at the end of the 1895 season. Still, Freedman also inadvertently managed to save the Giants from his own machinations when he hired fiery John McGraw in 1902. McGraw went on to manage the Giants for 31 seasons and led them to three World Series titles.

13 John T. Brush

Brush purchased the Giants from Andrew Freedman in 1902 after holding an interest in the team for more than 10 years. He was directly involved in Freedman's decision to hire John McGraw as manager and, once in charge, encouraged McGraw to go out and get the players he needed to build a champion. When the Giants won the National League pennant in 1904, he and McGraw refused to play the Boston Red Sox in the World Series because they considered the fledgling American League inferior. But when the Giants won the pennant again in 1905, Brush and McGraw agreed to play, and the Giants beat the Philadelphia Athletics, 4 games to 1. After fire destroyed the Polo Grounds in April of 1911, Brush financed the building of a new park on the same site. Brush passed away after the Giants won two more pennants, in 1911 and '12.

Joe McGinnity;
Luther Taylor, inset

14 The Iron Man

"Iron Man" Joe McGinnity started and won both games of a doubleheader three times in August of 1903. He completed all six games. In his seven seasons with the Giants, McGinnity won 151 games and posted a cumulative ERA of 2.38. He had his best year in 1904, when he compiled a 35–8 record with a 1.61 ERA. McGinnity was elected to the Hall of Fame in 1946.

15 Actions Speak Louder

His nickname is most assuredly politically incorrect in this day and age, but not back in the early 1900s. Luther "Dummy" Taylor, a deaf-mute, pitched for the Giants from 1900 to 1908, except for a brief stint in Cleveland in 1902. During that time, Taylor won 115 games, including a career-best 21 in 1904. With teammates Christy Mathewson and Joe McGinnity, the 1904 Giants became one of only seven teams in the National League since 1900 to have three 20-game winners in the same season. New York repeated the feat in 1905, 1913, and 1920.

"McGinnity was a magician in the box."

— Connie Mack

16 Christy Mathewson

The refined Bucknell graduate was as popular as any player in the early 1900s. Only Cy Young and Walter Johnson won more games in their careers than Mathewson. His 373 wins are tops in National League history, tied with Grover Alexander. Between 1903 and 1914, "Big Six" won 22 or more games each season. Four times he won 30 or more, including a career-best 37 in 1908.

Mathewson threw a blazing fastball, but his "fadeaway," similar to a screwball, was his signature pitch. Twice he threw no-hitters — in 1901 versus the Cardinals, and in 1905 versus the Cubs.

He was an original inductee into the Hall of Fame in 1936, receiving 91 percent of the vote from the Baseball Writers' Association. Somehow, 21 writers thought he didn't merit inclusion. Since no numbers were worn by players in Mathewson's era, the Giants retired the letters "NY" in his honor.

17 Shuttin' 'Em Down

In the 1905 Fall Classic versus the Philadelphia Athletics, Christy Mathewson pitched three shutouts in the span of six days. He won Game 1, 3–0, with a four-hitter. Mathewson tossed another four-hitter in Game 3, winning 9–0. And in Game 5, he threw a six-hitter, as the Giants won 2–0 and clinched their third world championship.

18 1.14

Christy Mathewson's 1.14 ERA in 1909 is a franchise and National League record.

"You can learn little from victory. You can learn everything from defeat."

— Christy Mathewson

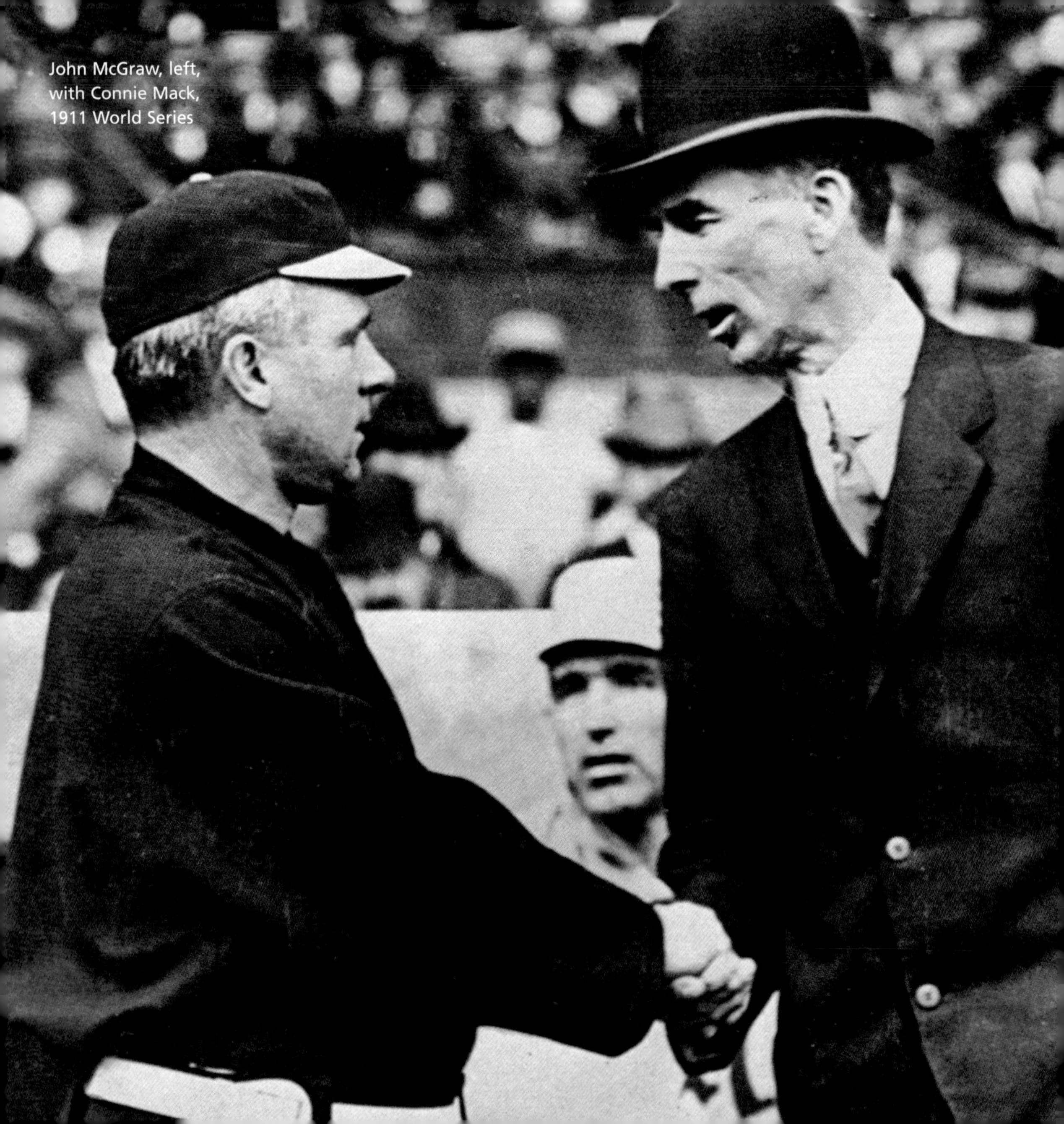

John McGraw, left, with Connie Mack, 1911 World Series

19 John McGraw

The feisty and fiery McGraw was the manager of the Giants for more than three decades. In his 31 years at the helm, starting in 1902, the Giants won 10 National League pennants and finished second 11 other times. Nicknamed "Little Napoleon" for his dictatorial manner, McGraw led the team to consecutive pennants in 1904 and '05, winning a World Series title in 1905. The Giants might have had another title, but in 1904, McGraw and owner John T. Brush refused to play the American League champions from Boston because they considered the league inferior. After four more pennant winners in 1911, '12, '13, and '17, the Giants set a National League record by winning four consecutive pennants from 1921 to 1924, and they won the World Series in '21 and '22, defeating the New York Yankees both times.

Regarded as a baseball genius and one of its most influential figures, McGraw had 2,840 wins as a manager, second only to the legendary Connie Mack. He was inducted into the Hall of Fame in 1937.

"One percent of ballplayers are leaders of men. The other ninety-nine percent are followers of women."

—John McGraw

20 Gem Dandy

It was July 4, 1908. Hooks Wiltse took the mound for the first game of a doubleheader against the Philadelphia Phillies at the Polo Grounds. For eight and two-thirds innings, Wiltse had a perfect game. But with two outs in the top of the ninth, his pitch brushed the arm of Phillies pitcher George McQuillan, ending his perfect game. Wiltse got the next batter, and the game went to the 10th inning tied at 0–0. Wiltse retired the side in order in the 10th and the Giants scored one in the bottom of the inning, giving Wiltse his no-hit gem. He's one of only four pitchers in major-league history to throw a 10-inning no-hitter. Wiltse won his first 12 decisions as a starter, in 1904, a major-league record.

21 Seeing Red

On opening day, 1909, Giants pitcher Red Ames held the Brooklyn Dodgers hitless for nine and one-third innings, but he eventually lost 3–0, in 13 innings. Brooklyn's Kaiser Wilhelm held the Giants to just three hits while recording the shutout victory. In 11 seasons with New York, Ames won 108 games and posted a cumulative ERA of 2.45, fourth best in franchise history.

22 Lucky 13

On May 13, 1911, the Giants scored 13 runs in the first inning, including seven before the first out was recorded. First baseman Fred Merkle had an inside-the-park home run and a double to drive in six in the inning, and the Giants went on to beat St. Louis 19–5.

George Burns

23 Good Fortune

Charlie "Victory" Faust talked his way onto the team in 1911 when he convinced manager John McGraw that a fortune-teller predicted a Giants pennant if Faust joined the team and pitched for them. McGraw put him on the roster, and though Faust made only two appearances, pitching two innings and giving up one earned run, the prediction came true as New York won the pennant by 7 1/2 games.

24 The Thieves

On August 8, 1909, outfielder Bill O'Hara stole second, third, and home in the eighth inning of a 3–0 Giants win over the St. Louis Cardinals. Ten days later, 49-year-old Arlie Latham stole second in a game versus the Philadelphia Phillies, becoming the oldest major-league player ever to steal a base.

On June 20, 1912, Josh Devore did something no one else ever has: he stole four bases in one inning. Devore came up twice in the ninth inning versus the Boston Beaneaters and singled both times. He proceeded to steal both second and third base each time, totaling five steals for the game in a 21–12 victory.

The swift George Burns stole home 28 times in his career, including five times in 1918. He set a modern-day Giants record with 62 stolen bases during the 1915 season.

25 Rube Marquard

For three years, 1911–13, Rube Marquard was just about as good a pitcher as anybody, and that's saying a lot, since he was a teammate of Christy Mathewson at the time. After a less-than-stellar start to his career, Marquard came into his own in 1911. He went 24–7 with a 2.50 ERA, and he led the league in strikeouts, with 237. His dominance continued in 1912 as he opened the season with 19 consecutive victories, tying former Giant Tim Keefe for the major-league record. He finished the year 26–11 and won Games 3 and 6 of the 1912 World Series against Boston. In 1913, Marquard posted a 23–10 record with a 2.50 ERA as the Giants won their third consecutive NL pennant. He added a no-hitter to his résumé in 1915, versus the archrival Dodgers. Marquard was inducted into the Hall of Fame in 1971.

Josh Devore, Larry Doyle, Rube Marquard, Art Devlin, Fred Merkle, and F.A. Devlin

26 It's Great to be Young and a Giant

Second baseman Larry Doyle spent 13 seasons in New York and was captain of the Giants from 1908 through 1916, helping lead the team to consecutive NL pennants in 1911, '12, and '13. "Laughing Larry" won the NL MVP award in 1912 with a career-best .330 batting average and 90 RBI. As an up-and-coming star on a powerhouse team, Doyle made his famous comment, "It's great to be young and a Giant."

Fred Snodgrass

27 The Muffin' Men

It's more of a lowlight than a highlight, but it's also an essential part of Giants lore. In 1912, the Giants won 103 games and their second straight National League pennant. They faced Hall of Famer Tris Speaker and the Boston Red Sox in the World Series. With the Series tied at 3 games apiece, plus one tie, the teams faced off in the finale on October 16. After the ninth ended in a 1–1 tie, the game went to extra innings. New York scored a run in the top of the 10th to take a 2–1 lead, but in the bottom of the inning, Clyde Engle's fly ball leading off the inning was dropped by Giants center fielder Fred Snodgrass for an error. After Snodgrass made a superb play to record the first out, Steve Yerkes walked, bringing up Speaker. Pitcher Christy Mathewson induced a foul pop out of Speaker, but the ball fell between first baseman Fred Merkle and catcher Chief Meyers when Mathewson called for Meyers to make the play, even though it appeared that Merkle was in a better position to catch it. Given a second chance, Speaker laced a single to score the tying run. After Mathewson walked Duffy Lewis to load the bases, Larry Gardner's sacrifice fly scored the winning run, giving the game and Series to Boston. The misplayed foul ball became known as "Merkle's Muff," and Snodgrass' error the "$30,000 Muff"— which was the difference between the winners' and losers' shares in the Series.

MERKLE, N. Y. NAT'L

28 The Big Chief

A Cahuilla Indian, John "Chief" Meyers played seven seasons with the Giants, catching Hall of Famers Christy Mathewson, Rube Marquard, and Joe McGinnity. He was a key member of the teams that won three consecutive National League pennants from 1911 to 1913. Meyers set a franchise record for catchers in 1910 with 154 assists. He batted .300 as a Giant.

29 Jim Thorpe

Thorpe spent part of six seasons with the Giants in 1913–19. An All-American in football and Olympic champion, he is regarded by many as the greatest American athlete of the 20th century. However, Thorpe's major-league career was somewhat less notable than his other sporting exploits. Thorpe posted a less-than-stellar .252 career batting average in just 289 games.

30 The Streakers

During the 1916 season, the Giants set two major-league records for consecutive wins, yet still managed to finish the season in fourth place. In May, New York won 17 consecutive games, all on the road, setting a record since tied by the 1984 Detroit Tigers. The Giants won an amazing 26 games in a row in September, but still finished seven games behind the first-place Dodgers.

Chief Meyers

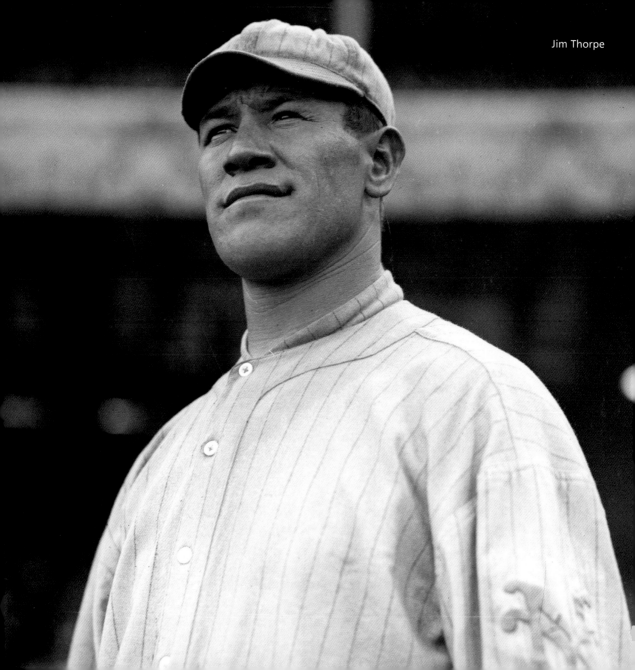
Jim Thorpe

George Kelly

31 Charles A. Stoneham

Stoneham, a stockbroker, purchased the Giants from Harry Hempstead in 1919, partnering with Francis X. McQuade and John McGraw. During his tenure, the Giants won four consecutive NL pennants from 1921 to 1924, winning the World Series in 1921 and '22, and added another world championship in 1933. Like earlier owner John T. Brush, Stoneham allowed McGraw to spend freely on personnel, and it showed in the success of the club. Stoneham died in 1936, and his son, Horace, took over the team.

32 Highpockets

First baseman George Kelly became the first Giants player to hit 20 home runs in a season when he led the National League with 23 in 1921. He added 21 long balls in 1924 and 20 more in 1925. Known as "Highpockets," the 6-foot-4 Kelly hit over .300 for six consecutive seasons, with a career-high .328 in 1922. In each of four straight years, he drove in more than 100 runs, with a career-best 136 in 1924. Kelly was inducted into the Hall of Fame in 1973.

"[Kelly made] more important hits for me than any player I ever had."

—John McGraw

33 Four for Four

In 1921, Frankie Frisch and mid-season acquisition Irish Meusel played key roles as the Giants won the first of four consecutive National League pennants. Jesse Barnes won two games in relief as the NL champions defeated the New York Yankees in the World Series, 5 games to 3.

The Giants won their second consecutive World Series title in 1922, again defeating the crosstown Yankees, 4 games to none with one tie. That year, Meusel, Casey Stengel, George Kelly, and Dave Bancroft led the way offensively, and Bancroft fielded an NL-record 984 chances at shortstop. On May 7, Jesse Barnes tossed a no-hitter against Philadelphia.

Frisch and Meusel led the Giants to a third straight NL title in 1923. Frisch batted .348 for the year, and Meusel drove in a league-leading 125 runs. In their third consecutive World Series versus the Yankees, the Giants lost 4 games to 2.

The Giants established a National League record in 1924 by winning their fourth consecutive pennant. First baseman Kelly led the way this time, batting .324 with 21 home runs and 136 RBI as the Giants edged the Brooklyn Dodgers by just a game and a half. Washington defeated the Giants 4 games to 3 in the World Series, winning Game 7, 4–3, in 12 innings.

Casey Stengel, Jimmy O'Connell, Ross Youngs, Bill Cunningham, and Irish Meusel

34 The Fordham Flash

In his eight seasons with the Giants, Frankie Frisch played on seven teams that finished first or second in the National League, including four pennant winners and two World Champions, in 1921 and '22. The "Fordham Flash" led the Giants in hitting four times, including a career-high .348 in 1923, and was tops in stolen bases for seven consecutive years, from 1920 to 1926. Frisch compiled a .363 batting average in 26 World Series games. Despite all that, the Giants chose to trade Frisch to the Cardinals after the 1926 season in exchange for Rogers Hornsby. Frisch was inducted into the Hall of Fame in 1947.

35 Stonewall Jackson's Army

An exceptional defensive shortstop who also had some pop, Travis Jackson joined John McGraw's Giants in 1922 as an 18-year-old. Between 1925 and 1927, the Giants roster included six infielders who would eventually become Hall of Famers: Jackson, first basemen George Kelly and Bill Terry, second basemen Frankie Frisch and Rogers Hornsby, and Fred Lindstrom at third. In 1930, Jackson, Terry, Lindstrom, and Hughie Critz formed the best-hitting infield in baseball history: Jackson hit a career-high .339, and the four combined to bat a composite .349. Jackson joined the Hall of Fame in 1982.

"His range was such that he played second base, some of center field, and a slice of right field, too."

— Damon Runyon on Frankie Frisch

Frankie Frisch

36 A Numbers Game

New York became the first team in the 20th century to score in every inning when it pasted Philadelphia 22–8 on June 1, 1923.

37 The Boy Wonder

The precocious teen Fred Lindstrom went 10 for 30 (.333) in the 1924 World Series versus the Washington Senators, including a four-for-five, two-RBI day against Hall of Famer Walter Johnson in Game 5. At only 18 years, 10 months, and 13 days, the "Boy Wonder" became the youngest player ever to appear in the World Series. He batted .300 or better for six consecutive years from 1926 to 1931, including a career-best .379 in 1930. In 1928, Lindstrom became the first National League player in the 20th century to total nine hits in a doubleheader, a record that remains unbroken. He was inducted into the Hall of Fame in 1976.

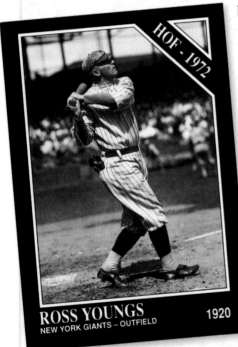

ROSS YOUNGS
NEW YORK GIANTS – OUTFIELD
1920

38 Ross Youngs

Giants manager John McGraw called Youngs "the greatest outfielder I ever saw." Youngs spent 10 seasons with the Giants, batting .300 or better nine times and compiling a .322 career average, third best in franchise history. His career was cut short in 1926 by a kidney disorder; Youngs died the next year at the age of 30. He was inducted into the Hall of Fame in 1972.

Fred Lindstrom

"He is a standout with me. Ott is the best-looking young hitter in my time with the Giants."

—John McGraw

39 Mel Ott

This "Boy Wonder," from Gretna, Louisiana, had a small frame — he was 5-foot-9, 170 pounds — and an unorthodox batting style, but Ott became one of the game's all-time greats, slugging 511 home runs and driving in a franchise-record 1,860 runs in his 22-year career with the Giants. Eight times Ott, who joined the team at the tender age of 17 in 1926, smashed 30 or more home runs, including a career-high 42 in 1929. For eight straight years, and nine out of 10, he drove in more than 100 runs, with a career-high 151, also in 1929.

In 1942, toward the end of his playing days, Ott replaced Bill Terry as player-manager of the Giants and remained at the helm into the 1948 season. In 1951, he was inducted into the Hall of Fame. His number, 4, has been retired by the Giants.

40 Memphis Bill

Name the last National Leaguer to hit .400 or better. Can't do it? It was the Giants' first baseman Bill Terry, back in 1930. His .401 average and 254 hits both led the league and are Giants records. After a three-game "cup of coffee" in 1923, "Memphis Bill" spent the next 13 years as a New York fixture. His .341 career batting average tops the Giants' record book, and his 2,193 hits are third all-time. When the great John McGraw decided to relinquish the managerial reins midway through the 1932 season, he turned to Terry as his successor. The very next year, player-manager Terry led the team to a World Series win over the Washington Senators. He took the Giants back to the Fall Classic in 1936 and '37, where they were defeated by the New York Yankees each time. Terry was inducted into the Hall of Fame in 1954. His number, 3, has been retired by the Giants.

41 Totally Offensive

Imagine a team these days batting better than .300 for the year but not winning the pennant. Well, back in the early days it happened quite a few times. In 1930, the entire National League batted .303, with the Giants leading the way with a record .319 team average. Still, they finished third, behind St. Louis (.314 team average) and Chicago (.309 team average) in the race for the National League pennant. Bill Terry led the way with a .401 mark. Fred Lindstrom hit .379, and Mel Ott chipped in with a .349 average.

"To hit .400 you need a great start and you can't have a slump. The year I did it … I was really hitting the ball on the nose."

— Bill Terry

Bill Terry

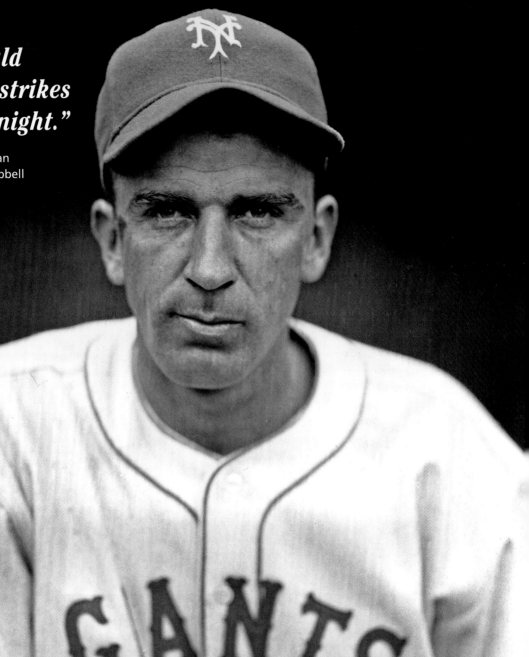

"He could
throw strikes
at midnight."

—Billy Herman
on Carl Hubbell

42 Carl Hubbell

Hubbell's nickname, "the Meal Ticket," is an obvious allusion to his dominance on the mound. One of the best left-handers ever, "King Carl" spent his entire 16-year career with the Giants, amassing the second-most wins (253) and innings pitched (3,590 1/3) in franchise history. His 36 shutouts rank third.

One of the few pitchers ever to master the screwball, Hubbell was 4–2 in three World Series with a 1.79 ERA, including a pair of complete-game wins over the Washington Senators in the 1933 Series, won by the Giants. He no-hit the Pittsburgh Pirates in 1929, and he threw an 18-inning shutout over the St. Louis Cardinals in the 1933 championship season, at one point also hurling a franchise-record 46 1/3 consecutive scoreless innings. From July 1936 through May 1937, Hubbell set a major-league record by winning 24 consecutive decisions. He gave up two or fewer runs in 20 of the 24 victories. Hubbell was inducted into the Hall of Fame in 1947. His number, 11, has been retired by the Giants.

43 Fanning the Famers

Over the course of the first two innings of the 1934 All-Star game at the Polo Grounds, Carl Hubbell fanned five future Hall of Famers in succession: Babe Ruth, Lou Gehrig, Jimmie Foxx, Al Simmons, and Joe Cronin.

44 High Fives

The Giants of 1939 were a prolific hitting team. On June 6, they hit five home runs in the fourth inning of a game versus the Cincinnati Reds at the Polo Grounds. The Giants hit a total of seven for the game in defeating the Reds 17–3. A couple of months later, they again hit seven homers in a game, as they thumped Philadelphia 11–2.

On August 23, 1961, the Giants once again victimized the Reds. Leading 2–0 entering the top of the ninth, the Giants put together a 12-run, 11-hit inning that featured another five home runs, winning by the final score of 14–0.

45 Big Bill

The Giants' Bill Voiselle is the only rookie in major-league history to win 20 games and lead the league in strikeouts when pitching at least 300 innings. In 1944, "Big Bill" led the National League with 161 strikeouts, posting a record of 21–16 in 312 2/3 innings.

46 Mine Goes to 11

Unheralded Phil Weintraub set a franchise record for RBI in a game when he knocked in 11, in a 26–8 drubbing of the archrival Dodgers on April 30, 1944. He had two doubles, a triple, a home run, and a bases-loaded walk for the day. Only Jim Bottomley (1924) and Mark Whiten (1993), both of the St. Louis Cardinals, ever drove in more (12) in a single game.

At right, Bobby Thomson, Willard Marshall, and Johnny Mize

47 The Windowbreakers

The 1947 Giants hit a record 221 home runs, easily eclipsing the mark of 182 previously held by the 1936 New York Yankees and earning them the nickname "the Windowbreakers." The team set a National League record by hammering 55 homers in July alone. Johnny Mize finished with 51 for the year, tying him for the league lead with Pittsburgh's Ralph Kiner.

48 Larry Jansen

Jansen opened his major-league career by posting a remarkable 21–5 record as a rookie in 1947. He won a career-high 23 games in 1951. But his greatest contribution may have come after his playing days. As the Giants pitching coach from 1961 to 1971, Jansen was instrumental in the development of Giants greats Juan Marichal, Gaylord Perry, and Cy Young award winner Mike McCormick.

49 Monte Irvin

Two years after Jackie Robinson broke baseball's color barrier in 1947, 30-year-old Monte Irvin and Hank Thompson became the first African Americans to play for the Giants, on July 8, 1949. A great all-around player, Irvin was a key part of the Giants' 1951 pennant-winning season, batting .312 with a team-best 24 homers and a league-leading 121 RBI. After an injury ended his 1952 season, Irvin came back to hit a major-league career-high .329 in '53 and added a World Series title to his résumé in 1954. Irvin was inducted into the Hall of Fame in 1973.

MONTE IRVIN
NEW YORK GIANTS

Monte Irvin,
Willie Mays, and
Hank Thompson

"*Nice guys finish last.*"
—Leo Durocher

Horace Stoneham, Bobby Thomson, and
Leo Durocher celebrate the 1951 pennant

50 Horace C. Stoneham

After his father, Charles, passed away in 1936, Horace Stoneham ran the franchise for 40 years and is regarded as its finest owner. He was both generous and insightful. He paid his players well and went in search of the best talent, signing Juan Marichal, the Alou brothers, and others from the talent-rich Dominican Republic. His controversial hiring of manager Leo Durocher from the Brooklyn Dodgers drew the ire of Giants fans, but the success that followed soon won them over. In 1957, convinced that New York couldn't support three teams, Stoneham announced that he was moving the Giants to San Francisco. He directed the club through its transition to the West Coast and stayed on as owner until 1975.

51 Leo Durocher

Durocher spent 17 years in the big leagues, mostly playing shortstop, and became the player-manager for the Dodgers in 1939. In 1948, when Giants owner Horace Stoneham requested permission to talk to Dodgers coach Burt Shotton about filling New York's managerial position, Dodgers owner Branch Rickey indicated he was willing to part with his combative manager, Durocher. Stoneham jumped at the chance, and "Leo the Lip" made the improbable, incomprehensible jump to the Giants from the archrival Dodgers in mid-season. Not only that, he replaced beloved Giants legend Mel Ott. New York fans were aghast, but Durocher rebuilt the struggling team. He directed the Giants' stunning 1951 comeback from 13 1/2 games down in August, as they defeated the Dodgers in a three-game playoff for the pennant on Bobby Thomson's "Shot Heard 'Round the World." The Giants lost to the Yankees in the World Series, but three years later, Durocher had the Giants back in the Fall Classic. This time, they would not be denied, sweeping the Indians 4 games to none. Durocher was elected to the Hall of Fame in 1994.

52 The Shot Heard 'Round the World

In Willie Mays' rookie year of 1951, Bobby Thomson moved from center field to third base to make room for Mays in center. In mid-August, the Giants trailed archrival Brooklyn by 13 1/2 games. But New York went on a 16-game winning streak, followed by a 12-and-1 run to finish the season that left the Giants in a dead heat with the Dodgers for the pennant. A three-game playoff ensued. After the teams split the first two games, the Dodgers carried a 4–1 lead into the bottom of the ninth in the third and final game, on October 3. Three hits off the Dodgers' Don Newcombe plated a run, cutting the deficit to 4–2, with runners at second and third and one out. Dodgers manager Charlie Dressen replaced Newcombe with Ralph Branca. Dressen and Branca decided not to intentionally walk Thomson and put the winning run on base, even though Thomson had 31 home runs on the year. After a first-pitch strike, Thomson lined Branca's second pitch into the left-field seats, sending the Polo Grounds crowd into a frenzy as the Giants won the game 5–4 and went on to the World Series. "The Shot Heard 'Round the World" remains one of the most dramatic moments ever in baseball.

"That homer raised me to a high level, with the top guys in the game."

— Bobby Thomson

53 The Giants Win the Pennant!

Russ Hodges' call of Bobby Thomson's 1951 "Shot Heard 'Round the World" is nearly as famous as the home run itself:

"One out, last of the ninth, Branca pitches. Thomson takes a strike called, on the inside corner…Brooklyn leads it 4 to 2. Hartung down the line at third, not taking any chances. Lockman without too big of a lead at second, but he'll be running like the wind if Thomson hits one. Branca throws, there's a long drive, it's gonna be, I believe…The Giants win the pennant! The Giants win the pennant! The Giants win the pennant! The Giants win the pennant! Bobby Thomson hits it into the lower deck of the left field stands! The Giants win the pennant and they're going crazy! … Oh-ho! I don't believe it! I don't believe it! I will not believe it!"

54 The Voices

Russ Hodges' call of Bobby Thomson's "Shot Heard 'Round the World" is his legacy, but he called many great moments as the voice of the Giants in a career that spanned four decades and two coasts. From 1949 in New York until his retirement in 1970 in San Francisco, Hodges broadcast home runs with his signature, "It's bye-bye, baby!"

Baritone Lon Simmons partnered with and then succeeded Russ Hodges as the voice of the Giants from 1958 to 1973, 1976 to 1978, and on a limited basis from 1996 to 2002. Hank Greenwald made the call with his entertaining manner in the '80s and '90s. And the silky smooth Jon Miller followed Greenwald behind the mike in 1997. Miller has become known throughout the country as ESPN's lead broadcaster for the network's nationally televised games.

Brooklyn's Andy Pafko watches Bobby
Thomson's home run clear the fence;
Russ Hodges, inset

315 FT.

55 The Barber

From July 1950 through May of 1952, Sal Maglie won 45 games for the Giants while losing only seven. Nicknamed "the Barber" for his tendency to give batters "close shaves" by pitching them high and tight, Maglie recorded four straight shutouts in 1950, with a streak of 45 consecutive scoreless innings. His 23 wins in 1951 led the National League. Maglie was the starting pitcher for the Giants when Bobby Thomson hit his historic "Shot Heard 'Round the World."

56 The Rivalry

Giants-Dodgers. It's a rivalry that has been around nearly as long as baseball has. The Giants and Dodgers first met as major-league teams way back in 1884 in an exhibition game won by the Giants, 8–0. Through the years, the two teams have faced off countless times—and crushed each other's dreams with an amazing regularity. The "Shot Heard 'Round the World" is the most famous example, and Juan Marichal's bat to John Roseboro's head in 1965 is the ugliest, but the list goes on and on. The Yankees and Red Sox may have a fiercer rivalry, but the Giants' and Dodgers' has been much more consistently competitive over the years.

"It was a pretty fierce rivalry....We didn't like them, and they didn't like us."

—Bobby Thomson

"*I think I was the best baseball player I ever saw.*"

—Willie Mays

57 Willie Mays

Mays is considered by many to be the greatest all-around player in the history of the game. His first major-league hit, a tremendous home-run blast off Warren Spahn, sailed out of the Polo Grounds in 1951. Mays went on to hit 20 home runs that year and win the NL Rookie of the Year award.

His 660 homers are fourth all-time in the majors. Mays also holds the Giants' all-time records for games played, runs scored, and hits. He's second in RBI.

The "Say Hey Kid" won two National League MVP awards, in 1954 and 1965. He hit .300 or better and recorded 100-plus RBI 10 times. Mays won 12 Gold Gloves, played in 24 All-Star games, and led the league in stolen bases four times. He was the first player to surpass both 300 home runs and 300 stolen bases.

Mays' over-the-shoulder catch of Vic Wertz' deep drive to center field in the 1954 World Series is regarded as one of baseball's greatest plays. In 1979, Mays was inducted into the Hall of Fame. His number, 24, has been retired by the Giants.

58 The Catch

It's become a legend. Game 1 of the 1954 World Series, September 29, the score was tied 2–2 in the top of the eighth inning, and the mighty Cleveland Indians, winners of a record 111 games that season, had men on first and second with none out. Vic Wertz ripped Don Liddle's pitch to deep center field. Willie Mays turned his back on the ball, sprinted toward the center-field wall, and made an improbable, spectacular over-the-shoulder catch and throw that saved two runs. The Indians failed to score, and the Giants went on to win the game and the Series. Mays later quipped, "I had it the whole time."

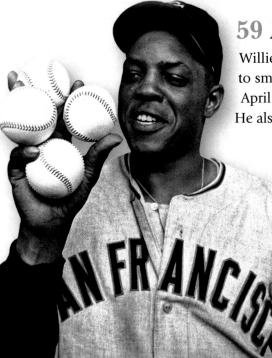

59 A 4-Gone Conclusion

Willie Mays became only the ninth player ever to smack four home runs in a single game, on April 30, 1961, versus the Braves in Milwaukee. He also had a San Francisco–record 8 RBI.

"As a batter, his only weakness is a wild pitch."

—Bill Rigney on Willie Mays

60 Take Me Home, Dusty Rhodes

James "Dusty" Rhodes' feats in the 1954 World Series are the stuff of legend. In Game 1, facing the prohibitive favorite Cleveland Indians, Rhodes pinch-hit for Monte Irvin in the bottom of the 10th inning with the game tied 2–2 and two men on base. Rhodes curled a Bob Lemon fastball just inside the foul pole and over the right-field fence for a home run and a 5–2 Giants

victory. In Game 2, again pinch-hitting for Irvin, Rhodes hit a bloop single in the fifth inning, scoring Mays and tying the game at 1. He added a solo home run in the seventh, and the Giants won 3–1. Rhodes had a two-run single in a 6–2 Game 3 win, and the Giants completed the sweep in Game 4. For the Series, Rhodes was four for six with seven RBI.

61 Westward, Ho!

When owner Horace Stoneham and his Giants headed west in 1958, after 75 years in New York, they were greeted by thousands and thousands of thrilled Bay Area residents. Major-league baseball had finally made it to the West Coast. While Candlestick Park was under construction, the team played in Seals Stadium in downtown San Francisco. The Giants won their first game in the beautiful little ballpark, 8–0, over the new Los Angeles Dodgers. The Giants moved out after just two years, when Candlestick Park was completed.

62 Orlando Cepeda

The "Baby Bull" joined the Giants in 1958, the same year they made the move from New York to San Francisco. Starting at first base in the Giants' first game in San Francisco, "Cha Cha" Cepeda homered in an 8–0 win over the Dodgers. His .312 average, 25 home runs, and 96 RBI earned him the 1958 National League Rookie of the Year award.

Cepeda had his best year in 1961, batting .311 with a career-high 46 homers and 142 RBI. He is sixth on the Giants' all-time list for home runs with 226 and 10th in RBI with 767. Cepeda went on to win the NL MVP award in 1967 while playing for the St. Louis Cardinals. He was inducted into the Hall of Fame in 1999 with a career batting average of .297, 379 home runs, and 1,365 RBI. The Giants retired his number, 30, in 1999.

"He is strong, he hits to all fields, and he makes all the plays."

—Willie Mays on Orlando Cepeda

63 The Stick

Candlestick Park, San Francisco's state-of-the-art baseball stadium, opened on April 12, 1960, to much fanfare. The highly anticipated event was filled with excitement, even though there were already many problems with the ballpark, the worst of which turned out to be completely beyond anyone's control—the weather. Over 42,000 fans showed up for the opening-day game, in which the Giants defeated the St. Louis Cardinals, 3–1. The winds quickly became the most discussed aspect of the park, and fog occasionally interrupted games. Even in midsummer, when temperatures approached 100 degrees not too far inland, Giants patrons could find themselves wrapped in blankets or wearing warm coats to protect themselves from the bitter winds blowing in off San Francisco Bay. The Giants spent 40 years in "the Stick" and never won a World Series. Maybe that alone was enough of a reason to move.

Beginning in 1983, Giants management issued commemorative pins, known as the "Croix de Candlestick," to fans who stayed until the sometimes bitter end of extra-inning night games. The pins featured a snowcapped SF logo and the words "Veni, Vidi, Vixi," meaning, "I came, I saw, I survived."

64 Well, Blow Me Down

Giants pitcher Stu Miller was called for a balk in the top of the ninth inning of the 1961 All-Star Game in Candlestick Park after a strong gust of wind caused him to move from his set position. The next day, the headline read, "Miller Blown Off Mound." The story was "blown" out of proportion, but it became a part of San Francisco lore.

"The greatest third baseman I ever saw."

—Bill Rigney on Jim Davenport

Jim Davenport;
Alvin Dark, inset

65 Jim Davenport

Davenport spent his entire 13-year playing career in San Francisco. Regarded by many as the best defensive infielder ever to play in San Francisco, he may be best remembered for his contribution at the plate in the 1962 three-game playoff with the Los Angeles Dodgers for the National League pennant. In the deciding game of the series, Davenport drew a bases-loaded walk that scored the go-ahead run in the top of the ninth inning as the Giants rallied from a 4–2 deficit to win 6–4. The victory gave the series to the Giants and brought San Francisco its first pennant.

66 Alvin Dark

A key addition to the Giants by manager Leo Durocher in 1950, Dark's steady presence at shortstop and strong bat helped propel New York to a National League pennant in 1951 and another pennant and World Series title in 1954. In 1961, Dark was named manager of the team, and though his controversial style ended his tenure after only four seasons, his .569 winning percentage is the best in San Francisco history. Dark directed the Giants to a 103-win season in 1962, but the pennant winners fell just short of another World Series title, losing Game 7 to the New York Yankees, 1–0.

"*He was awesome, easily the most feared hitter in the league.*"

—Don Sutton, from *Tales from the Giants Dugout*

67 Willie McCovey

Talk about making an impression: McCovey went four-for-four in his major-league debut, including two triples against Hall of Famer Robin Roberts of the Philadelphia Phillies, in July of 1959. Although he played in just 52 games that season, his .354 batting average and 13 home runs earned him National League Rookie of the Year honors.

With 36 homers and 105 RBI in 1968, and a career-high 45 dingers and 126 RBI in '69, "Stretch" became just the fifth player in baseball history to earn back-to-back home-run and RBI titles. He also batted .320 in 1969 and won the NL Most Valuable Player award.

McCovey hit 521 home runs in his career, 469 with the Giants, including an NL-record 18 grand slams. He combined with Willie Mays to form one of the most potent one-two punches in the history of the game.

It's not surprising that McCovey is one of the most beloved players ever to don a Giants uniform. At the end of a career that spanned four decades, the Giants retired his number, 44. McCovey was a first-ballot inductee into the Hall of Fame in 1986.

68 Oh, So Close

Had one game turned out differently, the last game, 1962 might have been known as the Year of Jack Sanford. After a so-so 6–6 start, right-hander Sanford went 18–1 the rest of the way, including a 16-game winning streak, to lead the Giants to their first pennant in San Francisco. The Giants made up four games on Los Angeles over the last seven games of the season to tie the Dodgers for the National League title with 101 wins apiece. The two teams split the first two games of a three-game playoff before the Giants ended the Dodgers' season with a four-run ninth-inning rally in Game 3 to win the pennant—on the eleventh anniversary of Bobby Thomson's "Shot Heard 'Round the World," no less.

In the World Series, facing the New York Yankees yet again, Sanford threw a three-hit shutout in Game 2 to even the Series at one game apiece. Over the next four games, the teams continued to trade victories, setting up a dramatic Game 7 showdown. Sanford took the mound for the third time in the Series, as the Yanks countered with ace Ralph Terry. After a bunt single by Matty Alou and a double by Willie Mays, the Giants had men on second and third with two outs in the bottom of the ninth, trailing 1–0—but Willie McCovey's sharp liner was snagged by second baseman Bobby Richardson to end the game, crushing the Giants' title hopes. The Yankees won the finale by scoring the only run on a double-play ball in the fifth inning.

SAN FRANCISCO GIANTS

"*I never pitched better in my life.*"

—Jack Sanford after Game 7, 1962

69 Thumbs Up

After defeating the Los Angeles Dodgers in a three-game playoff for the 1962 National League pennant, the Giants flew back to San Francisco, where a crowd estimated at somewhere between 50,000 and 100,000 waited to greet them. The team then boarded a bus that was to take it to Candlestick Park. When hysterical fans began to rock the bus, several players wanted no part of it and elected not to ride. Willie Mays managed to catch one of the few cabs available at the late hour. Many of the other players ended up hitching rides on Bayshore Freeway, including Juan Marichal and Orlando Cepeda.

70 Ain't It Grand

Sometimes it's just your turn to be in the spotlight. In the seventh inning of Game 4 of the 1962 World Series, Giants second baseman Chuck Hiller, a career .243 hitter with three homers on the year, lined Yankees reliever Marshall Bridges' fastball into the right-field seats for the first grand slam by a National Leaguer in World Series history. The Giants went on to win the game, 7–3, but the Yanks took the Series, 4 games to 3.

EC
16

Chuck Hiller

71 Juan Marichal

The "Dominican Dandy" made his major-league debut on July 19, 1960, at Candlestick Park and promptly threw a one-hit, 2–0 shutout of the Phillies. Marichal's high leg kick and delivery from three different arm angles made him nearly unhittable. From 1963 to 1969, Marichal won more than 20 games six times. He was 25–8 with a 2.41 ERA in '63, including a no-hitter against Houston. Marichal also threw a 16-inning shutout of Milwaukee, outpitching the great Warren Spahn in a 1–0 Giants win. In 1966, Marichal went 25–6, and won 26 more in '68. During the '60s, Marichal won more games than any other NL pitcher, yet, somehow, he never won the NL Cy Young award.

Marichal is tied for third in wins on the Giants' all-time list with 238, and second in games started (446), shutouts (52), and strikeouts (2,281). He was inducted into the Hall of Fame in 1983. His number, 27, has been retired by the Giants.

"He can throw all day within a two-inch space, in, out, up or down. I've never seen anyone as good as that."

—Hank Aaron

Jesus, Matty, and Felipe Alou

72 Uno, Dos, Tres

Brothers Felipe, Matty, and Jesus Alou played the outfield together in the eighth and ninth innings of a 13–5 win over the Pirates on September 15, 1963. It marked the first time that three siblings had played together in the same major-league outfield.

73 You Can Call Me Cy

In 1967, Mike McCormick led the league in wins, posting a 22–10 record, with a 2.85 ERA and five shutouts. Believe it or not, he is the only Giants pitcher ever to win the National League Cy Young award.

74 Gaylord Perry

Perry notched the first 134 of his 314 career wins while pitching for the Giants from 1962 to 1971. He won 21 games in 1966 and 23 in 1970, a year that included five shutouts and 23 complete games. Four times he struck out more than 200 batters, including 233 in 1969. His signature pitch was the spitball, which he continued to throw surreptitiously even though baseball had made it illegal way back in the 1920s. In 1967, Perry threw 40 consecutive scoreless innings, and in '68, he no-hit St. Louis. Perry also was the winning pitcher with 10 innings of shutout relief in an 8–6 win over the New York Mets in 23 innings in 1964. He was elected to the Hall of Fame in 1991.

75 Oh, No You Don't

On September 17, 1968, the Giants' Gaylord Perry no-hit the Cardinals, besting Bob Gibson 1–0 on Ron Hunt's first-inning home run. The next day, the Cardinals' Ray Washburn exacted revenge by no-hitting the Giants. It was the first time no-hitters had been thrown back-to-back in the same ballpark.

Gaylord Perry and Ray Washburn

"Gaylord was fantastic, simply fantastic."
—Gabe Paul

Commissioner Bowie Kuhn with Bobby Bonds,
1973 All-Star Game MVP

76 Bobby Bonds

Bobby Bonds, Barry's father, was a great player in his own right. His first career hit, a grand slam, came in the sixth inning of his first game with the Giants, June 25, 1968, at Candlestick Park. In 1970, Bonds batted a career-best .302 and scored 134 runs. He launched 39 round-trippers in 1973 and stole more than 40 bases in five of his six full seasons with the Giants. Bonds is one of only four players in baseball history to amass at least 300 home runs and 300 stolen bases, sharing that rare air with his son Barry, Willie Mays, and Andre Dawson.

77 Barr None

In his first full season with the Giants, in 1972, pitcher Jim Barr retired 41 consecutive hitters over a two-game span, setting a major-league record. Barr retired the last 21 Pittsburgh hitters he faced on August 23, recording a two-hit shutout. Six days later, he sent the first 20 St. Louis batters he faced back to the dugout without a hit, before Bernie Carbo finally ended the incredible streak with a double. Barr also won that game, with a three-hit shutout.

78 Staying Put

After a couple of other deals fell through, including one that would have moved the team to Toronto, Giants board member Bob Lurie and Bud Herseth, a meat-packer from Arizona, came up with the money to buy the team in 1976 and keep it in San Francisco. Lurie hired Al Rosen as general manager and Roger Craig as manager late in 1985, and the team immediately turned itself around. Just two years after losing a franchise-worst 100 games, the Giants won NL West Division titles in 1987 and again in '89.

John Montefusco

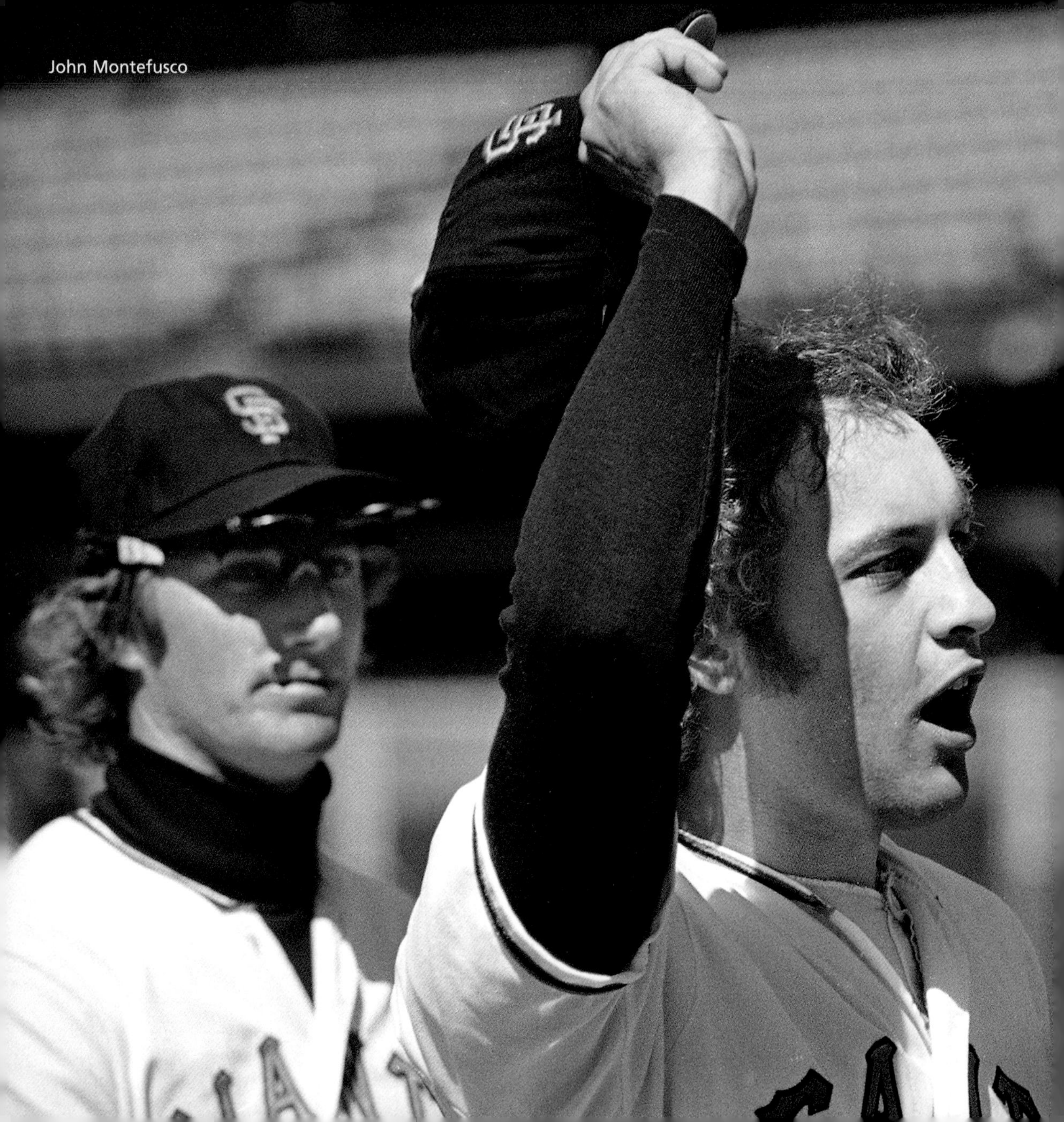

79 The Count of Montefusco

John "the Count" Montefusco was not one to go about his business quietly. He said what was on his mind and pitched with the same devil-may-care attitude. In his rookie season of 1975, he finished 15–9 with a 2.88 ERA and 215 strikeouts (second in the league), and he won the NL Rookie of the Year award. The following year, he made good on his own prediction when he no-hit the Braves, in a 9–0 victory in Atlanta.

80 Jack the Ripper

Jack Clark put together a San Francisco–record 26-game hitting streak in 1978, the third longest in franchise history, on his way to a .306 average. In 1982, he plated a franchise-record 21 game-winning RBI. From 1978 to 1983, "the Ripper" smashed 20 or more home runs every year, except for the strike-shortened season of 1981.

81 Moon Man

Greg Minton established a major-league record when, from September 6, 1978, through May 2, 1982, he pitched 269.1 consecutive innings without yielding a single home run. Known as the Moon Man for his zany antics, Minton is fourth on the Giants' all-time saves list, with 125.

82 Boo Who?

In response to fans jeering him for his poor play, Johnnie Lemaster had the word "Boo" stitched onto the back of his jersey in place of his name. Giants faithful lovingly gave Lemaster the nickname "Johnnie Disaster."

Johnnie Lemaster

83 The Crazy Crab

The Crazy Crab, an offshoot of the popular San Diego Chicken and Philly Phanatic, introduced by Giants management in 1984, was meant to be an anti-mascot. Fans were initially encouraged to boo him, but as the team stumbled through a 96-loss season, the crab became the target of anger and frustration as fans hurled epithets and various objects at him. The players even joined in the abuse. Crazy Crab was retired after just one season.

84 The Thrill

Will "the Thrill" Clark came to play and made no bones about it. In his first major-league at bat, "the Thrill" homered to straightaway center field off Hall of Famer Nolan Ryan. In 1987, his second season with the Giants, Clark hit .308 and hammered a career-high 35 homers as he led the Giants to the playoffs just two years after they had lost 100 games. Two years later, the team was back in the playoffs and Clark was the NLCS MVP, as San Francisco defeated the Cubs for the NL pennant.

Will Clark

85 The Worth of a Man

His story may seem tragic, but Dave Dravecky wouldn't describe it that way. After five-plus seasons with the San Diego Padres, Dravecky joined the Giants during the 1987 campaign. He posted a 7–5 record in 18 starts as a Giant and pitched a two-hit shutout of the Cardinals in Game 2 of the NLCS. Arthroscopic surgery in June of the following year ended his 1988 season. A malignant tumor was discovered in his pitching arm later that year and surgery was performed, removing the tumor and half his deltoid muscle. Doctors indicated it would take a miracle for Dravecky to pitch again. Undaunted, Dravecky worked his way back, and on August 10, 1989, he pitched eight innings in a 4–3 win over the Cincinnati Reds. Five days later, in his next start in Montreal, the humerus bone in Dravecky's arm snapped while he was throwing a pitch. Two months after the first break, his arm was again broken as the Giants celebrated their NLCS victory over the Cubs. Doctors eventually had to amputate his arm to prevent the spread of the cancer. Dravecky's baseball career was over, but he and his wife, Jan, formed Dave Dravecky's Outreach of Hope, a nonprofit ministry for "suffering people, especially those with cancer and amputation." Dravecky is the author of several books, including *The Worth of a Man*, which recounts his personal journey.

"Growing up I had two heroes, Sandy Koufax and Vida Blue ... All I cared about as a little kid was that I wanted to throw a baseball like they did."

— Dave Dravecky

86 Kevin Mitchell

Mitchell won the National League MVP award in 1989, becoming the first Giant to do so since Willie McCovey in 1969. In leading San Francisco to its first NL pennant since 1962, "Mitch" pounded out a league-leading 47 home runs and 125 RBI and had a slugging percentage of .635 while batting .291. Mitchell hit .353 with two home runs in the Giants' win over the Chicago Cubs in the '89 NLCS.

87 Roger Craig

Craig took over the Giants' managerial reins in late 1985. The team he inherited went on to lose 100 games for the first time in franchise history, 88 before Craig got there. But two years later, Craig had completely rebuilt the team, and his "Humm Baby" crew won the National League West Division title in a remarkable turn-around. Craig led the Giants to another West Division crown in 1989, and they went on to win the pennant by defeating the Chicago Cubs 4 games to 1. The Giants fell to the Oakland Athletics in the earthquake-delayed '89 World Series.

Kevin Mitchell

Roger Craig

88 1989 — All Shook Up

With Kevin Mitchell and Will Clark leading the way offensively, and pitchers Rick Reuschel and Scott Garrelts combining for 31 wins and only 13 losses, the Giants won their second NL West title in three years.

The Giants quickly dispatched the Chicago Cubs in the 1989 National League Championship Series, outslugging the Cubs and winning the series 4 games to 1. But after hammering the Cubs' pitching, the Giants' bats suddenly went silent in the first two games of "the Bay Bridge Series" versus Oakland. The Athletics' Dave Stewart opened the Series with a 5–0, five-hit shutout, and Oakland's Mike Moore followed that with a 5–1 four-hitter in Game 2.

When a 7.1-magnitude earthquake shook the Bay area about 30 minutes prior to the start of Game 3 on October 17, collapsing a section of the Bay Bridge, other roadways, and numerous buildings, and killing more than 60 people, baseball suddenly took a back seat to more serious matters.

Ten days later the World Series resumed, and Oakland finished what it had started, defeating the Giants in Games 3 and 4 to complete the sweep. It was a disappointing end to the Giants' first visit to the Fall Classic since 1962.

Rick Reuschel

Matt Williams

89 Closing Acts

Rod "Shooter" Beck smashed the Giants' single-season mark for saves by recording 48 in 1993, including 24 straight without a blown opportunity. In 1994, Beck completed all 28 save opportunities he had, and he extended that streak to 41 consecutive saves without a blown opportunity early in the 1995 season. Beck finished his Giants career with 199 total saves, second only to Rob Nen, who succeeded Beck in the closer role.

"Rapid Rob" Nen proceeded to surpass Beck's total in just five years of work. Nen recorded 40 or more saves in four of those five seasons, finishing his Giants career with a franchise-best 206. In the 2002 postseason, Nen recorded seven saves as the Giants fell one game short of winning their first World Series in nearly 50 years.

90 What Might Have Been

Giants third baseman Matt Williams had already hit 43 home runs in 112 games when a players' strike ended the 1994 season. He was on pace to hit 62 for the season and break Roger Maris' 33-year-old record of 61, but it was not to be. Williams hit 247 homers in his 10 seasons with the Giants. His two-run blast in a memorable 12-pitch at bat in Game 4 of the 1989 NLCS helped propel the Giants to their first pennant since 1962.

91 A Team of Dustiny

Brian Johnson's legendary leadoff homer in the bottom of the 12th inning off Dodgers reliever Mark Guthrie gave the Giants a two-game sweep of the late-season series and tied the teams for the division lead in September 1997. The Giants pulled away as the season drew to a close, and the "team of Dustiny"—so called because of the leadership of manager Dusty Baker— went on to a West Division crown.

Dusty Baker shares his feelings with umpire Mark Hirschbeck.

92 Dusty Baker

Baker was hired as Giants manager in 1993, after several years as a coach and hitting instructor. In 10 seasons, his teams won 840 games, making him the winningest manager in San Francisco history, and second on the franchise list behind John McGraw. The affable Baker was consistently able to get the most out of all of his players, and that led to repeated success. In his first season at the helm, the Giants won a franchise-record-tying 103 games, yet fell one game short of the division title. His teams won division titles in 1997 and 2000, but lost a one-game playoff to the Chicago Cubs for the final post-season spot in 1998. In 2002, Baker led his wild-card Giants to the National League pennant before they lost the World Series in heartbreaking fashion to the Anaheim Angels in seven games. Baker was named Manager of the Year three times in his 10-year tenure.

93 Barry Bonds

Love him or hate him, there's no denying Barry Bonds has put up Hall of Fame numbers — even before he was surrounded by scandal. Through 1998, generally agreed as the years before steroid use became common, Bonds hit 30 or more home runs in eight seasons. In 1993, his first year with the Giants, he hit 46 home runs while batting .336. In 1998, he became the first player in baseball history to record 400 home runs and 400 stolen bases. He has now surpassed 500 in both those categories.

The son of Giants great Bobby Bonds, and the godson of Willie Mays, Bonds flanked his record-setting year of 2001, in which he set the all-time single-season home-run record with 73, by hitting 49 in 2000, then smashing 46, 45, and 45 in the three years following 2001. To go along with his 46 long balls in 2002, Barry batted a career-best .370, and in 2004, he had a staggering .609 on-base percentage that included a major-league-record 232 walks.

So put an asterisk by his name and numbers if you must, but there's no denying that Barry Bonds is one of the greatest ever to play the game.

*"It's called talent.
I just have it.
I can't explain it.
You either have it
or you don't."*

—Barry Bonds

"You can build a team around Jeff. He's that good. He's the best offensive second baseman I have ever seen."

—Kevin Mitchell

Jeff Kent

94 Jeff Kent

From 1997 to 2002, Kent and Barry Bonds formed the best one-two punch the Giants have had since the days of Mays and McCovey. A solid second basemen with rare power, Kent hit 175 home runs in six seasons in San Francisco and knocked in 100-plus runs each year. In 2000, Kent edged Bonds for the NL MVP award, batting .334 with 33 homers and 125 RBI. His career-high 37 round-trippers and .313 average were keys to the Giants' success in 2002. While Giants fans may no longer hold Kent in such high esteem since his dubious exit after the 2002 season, he remains among the best to ever don a San Francisco uniform.

95 Peter Magowan

When owner Bob Lurie couldn't secure public funding for a new ballpark, he decided to sell the Giants to a group that was planning to move the

team to Tampa. Enter Peter Magowan, grandson of Merrill Lynch co-founder Charlie Merrill. Magowan grew up in New York and attended Giants games at the Polo Grounds as a kid. He put together a deal in 1993 that kept the Giants in San Francisco, and in 1995 his plans to build a new ballpark without any public financing were introduced. Magowan's vision, Pac Bell Park, opened in 2000 to great acclaim.

Felipe Alou, left, and Peter Magowan

"The view from the worst seats in the house still gives you a view of the Bay Bridge and the marina."

—Peter Gammons

96 AT&T Park

The Giants moved into their beautiful new ballpark as the 2000 season began. Initially known as Pac Bell Park, the ballpark was inspired by the legendary Wrigley Field and Fenway Park, and modeled after modern-day stadiums Camden Yards in Baltimore and Jacobs Field in Cleveland. A nine-foot statue of Giants great Willie Mays welcomes fans at the main entrance, and the area beyond the right-field bleachers, where home-run balls occasionally splash, is known as McCovey Cove, named after another Giants great, Willie McCovey. Hordes of fans in boats and kayaks patrol the cove for the buoyant souvenirs.

AT&T Park is the result of owner Peter Magowan's vision and dedication. It's the first major-league ballpark to be constructed without public financing since Dodger Stadium in 1962. Sports columnist Peter Gammons wrote, "As great as Camden Yards, Turner Field, The Jake and Coors Field are, this is the best fan's ballpark…"

J.T. Snow pulls Darren Baker
out of harm's way.

97 Those Darn Rally Monkeys

A 25–8 stretch run got the Giants into the 2002 playoffs as the National League wild card. After the Giants had dispatched the Atlanta Braves in the 2002 National League Division Series and the St. Louis Cardinals in the NLCS, they faced the Anaheim Angels in the World Series — their first appearance in the Fall Classic since 1989. Barry Bonds homered in his first World Series at bat, as the Giants won Game 1, 4–3. San Francisco dropped the next two games before winning Games 4 and 5 to take a 3-games-to-2 lead in the Series. Game 5, a 16–4 rout by the Giants, was made more memorable when J.T. Snow pulled 3 1/2-year-old batboy Darren Baker, Dusty Baker's son, out of harm's way as David Bell barreled home from third base.

In Game 6, the Giants had the Series in their grasp, leading 5–0 with one down in the bottom of the seventh. San Francisco was eight outs away from clinching the Series, but Angels fans were madly swinging their "rally monkeys" — a plush-toy mascot — in hopes of inspiring another late-inning comeback. The Angels responded by scoring three runs in the bottom of the seventh and three more in the bottom of the eighth, to win, 6–5, knotting the Series at 3 games apiece. Anaheim's newfound momentum carried over into Game 7, as the Angels defeated the Giants 4–1, ending San Francisco's hopes for its first World Series title since 1954.

"Your heart is heavy, your stomach is empty."

—Dusty Baker, from *Tales from the Giants Dugout*

98 A 16K Gem

On June 6, 2006, Giants pitcher Jason Schmidt equaled Christy Mathewson's 102-year-old franchise record for strikeouts in a game by fanning 16 Florida Marlins, including the last three, in a 2–1 Giants win.

99 715

With a full count and one man on base in the fourth inning, Barry Bonds launched a Byung-Hyun Kim fastball 445 feet into the center-field stands at San Francisco's AT&T Park for home run number 715. The May 28, 2006, blast moved Bonds past the immortal Babe Ruth and into second place on the all-time list behind Henry Aaron, who hit 755.

"For the fans of San Francisco, it can't get any better than this—even though I made them wait longer than I have in the past."

—Barry Bonds, from ESPN.com

Jason Schmidt

Benito Santiago, center, 2002 NLCS MVP,
celebrating with teammates

100 21 Pennants

In their 120-plus years of existence, the Giants
have won 21 National League pennants, in 1888,
1889, 1904, 1905, 1911, 1912, 1913, 1917, 1921, 1922,
1923, 1924, 1933, 1936, 1937, 1951, 1954, 1962, 1989,
2002, and 2010.

101 8 World Championships
1888, 1889, 1905, 1921, 1922, 1933, 1954, and 2010. At last!

1954 World Series, New York vs.
Cleveland, the Polo Grounds

Jason Schmidt receiving congratulations from his teammates for his record-tying 16-strikeout performance, June 6, 2006

Acknowledgments

First and foremost, a special word of thanks goes out to Jennifer Levesque, Leslie Stoker, Kate Norment, and the rest of the folks at Stewart, Tabori & Chang for their ongoing support. And to copy editor Richard Slovak, who also makes sure all the little facts and figures are correct. They manage the process with skill and ease.

I would also like to thank art director Mary Tiegreen, who conceived this series of books, and her husband, Hubert. I couldn't ask for better friends. Over the years we've become family.

To Kevin O'Sullivan at AP Wide World, and Pat Kelly at the National Baseball Hall of Fame Library, thank you for all your time and effort. The images in these books are what make them really special.

To Giants fans and baseball fans in general, from New York to California and everywhere in between, it's a great bond that we share with our love for this game. Treasure the moments, both bitter and sweet. The game will reward your devotion.

And, finally, to my team—they are treasures I truly cherish—my beautiful and ever-supportive wife, Mary; gorgeous and amazingly talented daughter, Savannah; handsome and brilliant son, Dakota; and good pal Sam, the dog, who slumbers through the occasional epithets I hurl at my computer; my parents, Ron and Beth, whom I see all too rarely and never for long enough; my brother, Ron, author of the companion Dodgers book, who played all the roles of big brother so well— tutor, tormentor, idol, and friend; my sister, Edie, who always makes me smile; and the rest of the Green, McGlone, and Mathwich clans—you're the best.

 **A Tiegreen Book**

Published in 2007 by Stewart, Tabori & Chang
An imprint of Harry N. Abrams, Inc.

Library of Congress Cataloging-in-Publication Data

Green, Dave, 1959-
  101 reasons to love the Giants /
by David Green.
    p. cm.
    ISBN-13: 978-1-58479-566-7
    ISBN-10: 1-58479-566-2
  1. San Francisco Giants (Baseball team)—Miscellanea.
  2. New York Giants (Baseball team)—Miscellanea. I. Title.
  II. Title: One hundred one reasons to love the Giants. III.
  Title: One hundred and one reasons to love the Giants.

GV875.S34G74 2007
796.357'640979461--dc22
2006028602

Text copyright © 2007 David Green
Compilation copyright © 2007 Mary Tiegreen

Editor: Jennifer Levesque
Designer: David Green, Brightgreen Design
Production Manager: Alexis Mentor

101 Reasons to Love the Giants is a book in the 101 REASONS TO LOVE™ Series.

101 REASONS TO LOVE™ is a trademark of Mary Tiegreen and Hubert Pedroli.

Printed and bound in China
10 9 8 7 6 5 4 3 2 1

HNA ▮▮▮▮▮
harry n. abrams, inc.
a subsidiary of La Martinière Groupe

115 West 18th Street
New York, NY 10011
www.hnabooks.com

Photo Credits

Pages 1, 6 (inset), 7, and 14-15 courtesy of the National Baseball Hall of Fame Library

Pages 2-3, 26, 38, 41, 42-43, 46, 47 (inset), 49, 50, 51, 53, 55, 56, 58, 59, 61, 61 (inset), 63, 64, 65 (inset), 66, 67, 69, 70, 71, 72-73, 74, 75 (inset), 76, 79, 81, 82, 83, 84, 86-87, 88, 90, 92, 93, 94, 95, 96, 97, 98, 99, 100, 102-103, 104, 106, 107 (inset), 108, 109 (inset), 110, 112 (inset), 113, 114-115, 116-117, and 118 courtesy of AP/Wide World Photos

Pages 5 (card), 8, 22, 44 (card), 54 (card), 59 (ball), 68 (card), 72 (pin), 77 (card), 78 (card), and 85 (ball) courtesy of David Green, Brightgreen Design

Pages 9 (inset), 12-13 (cards), 17, 20, 23 (inset), 24-25, 29, 30, 31 (card), 32, 33, 34, 35 (card), 36, 37, 45, and 120 (card) courtesy of the Library of Congress Prints and Photographs Division

Page 11 courtesy of Mary Tiegreen

Page 19 courtesy of Andy Jurinko

MATHEWSON, N. Y. NAT'L